Our Fingerprints
Spiral
Like Galaxies

Our Fingerprints Spiral Like Galaxies

Kimo RedeR

REGENT PRESS
Berkeley, California
2023

Copyright © 2023 by John Reder

[paperback]
ISBN 13: 978-1-58790-673-2
ISBN 10: 1-58790-673-2

[e-book]
ISBN 13: 978-1-58790-674-9
ISBN 10: 1-58790-674-0

Library of Congress Control Number: 2023946991

Front Cover Art
The front cover art is a colorized engraving from Isaac Holland's 1667 alchemical treatise *Die Hand der Philosophen*.

Back Cover Art
The back cover art includes a Mogollon-style handprint from the Three Rivers Petroglyph Site near Sierra Blanca, New Mexico.

Manufactured in the U.S.A.
Regent Press
Berkeley, CA
www.regentpress.net

This book is dedicated
to my wife Twink
and her own hands'
daily frolics and explorations.

<><><><><><><><><><><><><><><>
Ж Ж Ж Ж Ж Ж Ж Ж Ж Ж Ж
0 0 0 0 0 0 0 0 0 0 0 0 0 0 0 0 0 0 0
****
☼☼☼☼☼☼☼☼☼☼☼☼☼☼☼
∴∴∴∴∴∴∴∴∴∴∴∴∴∴∴∴
∧∧∧∧∧∧∧∧∧∧∧∧∧∧∧∧∧∧∧∧∧∧∧∧∧∧
▱▱▱▱▱▱▱▱▱▱▱▱▱▱▱▱▱▱▱▱▱▱▱
≈∞≈∞≈∞≈∞≈∞≈∞≈∞≈∞≈∞≈∞
«±«±«±«±«±«±«±«±«±«±«±«±«±«±«
ʃʃʃ
❉⋮❉⋮❉⋮❉⋮❉⋮❉⋮❉⋮❉⋮❉⋮❉⋮❉⋮❉⋮❉⋮❉⋮❉⋮
ʠʠʠʠʠʠʠʠʠʠʠʠʠʠʠʠʠʠʠʠʠʠʠʠʠʠ
+++++++++++++++++++++++++++
)))))))))))))))
d̉≥d̉≥d̉≥d̉≥d̉≥d̉≥d̉≥d̉≥d̉≥d̉
****
ℑʃaʃℑʃaʃℑʃaʃℑʃaʃℑʃaʃℑʃaʃℑʃaʃ
††††††††††††††††††††††††††††††††††††††
#############################
::
∞∞∞∞∞∞∞∞∞∞∞∞∞∞∞∞∞∞∞∞∞

The human hand generally has one bone for each letter in the Roman alphabet, as if its undergirding were imitating one of its own outputs. Our fingers feature fourteen phalanges that correspond to the fourteen lines of a standard sonnet, and indeed our hands can be read and interpreted just as sonnets can.

"Manual" as an adjective concerns the hand
    and "manual" as a noun refers to a how-to guide,
        but a "handbook" is not necessarily a "hand book"
            unless its subject matter mirrors
        what manipulated and manufactured it into being.

If God's finger passing the vital spark to Adam's finger on the Sistine Chapel ceiling is the direct current of divine motivation, the Wicked Witch of the West's fingers being electrocuted when touching Dorothy's ruby slippers in *The Wizard of Oz* is the alternating current of Not-Kansas-Anymore.

The "pen" in "pentagram" comes from the Greek pan for "all"
    and refers to the pen-wielding and all-containing hand:
        a five-rayed carbon-based star
        created from the crucible of an exploded star.

The word "hand" is always in subliminal rhyme with "spanned" and "band" and is indeed one of our main bridges spanning from Self to Other. Conversely, the word "hand" is also always in implied rhyme with "canned" as a matter of self-containment and "fanned" as a matter of self-relief.

In the lexicon of manual utterance
    hands held overhead mean "hostage" at a bank robbery
        and "hallelujah" at a Baptist choir practice
            and "humming silently" at a Bhakti yoga center.

Ж Ж Ж Ж Ж Ж Ж Ж Ж Ж

Marshall McLuhan referred to unexplored artistic spaces "where the hand of man has never set foot," and as a multimedia visionary he was also interested in that territory where the taste buds can hear and the tongue seeks to eavesdrop on the retina's sense of smell. As well, McLuhan only read so-called serious books "on the right-hand side" to avoid the inevitable redundancy and repetition he found on their flipsides.

The papillary friction ridges of human fingertips
are like a blend of homegrown corduroy
and a beerhall accordion's bellows
and the corrugated tin of a toolshed:
as composite in Texture as they are in Task.

The 80 Percent Recurrence:
4 out of 5 madonna paintings
cradle their infant with their left hand,
just as 4 out of 5 of our fingers are non-opposable
and 4 out of 5 bacterial infections are spread by hand.

A trial jury in which the foreman's hands are twiddling and the alternates' hands are white-knuckled is less likely to convict in a case of felony procrastination. In such a case, a prosecutor's hand-gestures jab and chop where a defender's wave and cup and a prosecutor's feet lunge and dart where a defender's sashay and backtrack.

 {}

According to Henry Dreyfuss' five-point approach to industrial design, Safety is the pinkie, Utility the ring finger, Maintenance the middle finger, Quality the index finger, and Appearance the thumb. In such a scheme, a fist is presumably a labor union huddling together as a strategic singularity.

To offset our logically standard "rules of thumb"
    tea parties have etiquette-enforcing "rules of pinkie"
   soccer games have etiquette-undoing "rules of middle finger"
       and fists have "rules of gavel"
    to overrule an open palm's pacifist objections.

The gypsy jazz guitarist Django Reinhardt lost the feeling in two fingers in a fire caused by celluloid flowers, but in an act of cross-species forgiveness still managed to perform several odes to actual blossoms, from "Honeysuckle Rose" to "Lilly Belle May June" to "Fleur D'Ennui."

Our fingers differ in base temperature and class temperament,
from the upper-crust cool of the pinkie
to the volatile swagger of the middle finger
to the phlegmatic subservience of the thumb.

****

The V of the Roman numeral system is a pictogram
of the gap between thumb and forefinger
using the web between those two digits as a trampoline
to pivot from an A-okay blessing to a more accusatory jab.

There are 31 possible combinations of the four fingers and the thumb according to an experimental film by Bruce Nauman, one for each day of a long month as if such hand-gestures were megaliths in an altar to the moon.

In Turkey, Kurdish farmers bargain during a non-stop handshake until an agreement is reached, treating one another's hands like udders milked into mutual satisfaction.

If our hands could taste like an octopus' skin can
   would a marble tabletop register as a dairy product
     and an unvarnished oak desktop as a fermented grain
      and a Formica countertop as loaded with artificial glutamates?

We "pare" the cuticles across a "pair" of hands, forming crescent-shaped debris evoking the waning moons prayed to by our pagan ancestors.

What would Mona Lisa's initial hand-gesture be
   if she could unfreeze herself from her now-iconic pose:
     a wiping of her finely shaded brow
      or a cracking of her demurely extended knuckles?

On a typewriter, our profane and
    ever-poised-to-strike middle finger
        suitably presses the "c" in "curse-word"
            the "d" in "damnable"
                and the "e"'s in "epithet."

The teacup handshake arches the hand to avoid palm-to-palm contact, perhaps because caffeine is known to increase the sweat of said palm. The "lobster claw" handshake is similarly performed mincingly with the thumb and fingertips: variations on this gesture named for other crustaceans await their own recognition, including the Blue Crab Back-Slap and the Crawdaddy Cuticle Clasp.

            ·:·|·:·|·:·|·:·|·:·|·:·|·:·|·:·|·:·|·:·|·:·|·:·

When one's right hand is Ptolemaic and
    one's left hand is Copernican
        managing a steering-wheel is an exercise
            in balancing two different senses of rotation
        and typing out a manuscript can go
            from geocentric to heliocentic in the tap of shift-key.

A video-game console awaits adolescent hands with less poise and patience than a chisel awaits a summer-vacation sculptor and with more eagerness and abandon than a divorce agreement awaits its dueling signatories.

Darwin cited the eye as divinely sublime, while Newton cited the thumb, perhaps because of Darwin's thumb-resembling nose nearly getting him taken off the Beagle voyage and Newton's lifetime virginity never finding the apple of his eye and despite Newton's work on optics and Darwin's insights into the development of the primate fingers.

There are no actual muscles inside the fingers,
and so our digital dexterity is a matter of remote-controlled
tendons that permit our palms to play puppeteer.

∧∧∧∧∧∧∧∧∧∧∧∧∧∧∧∧∧∧∧∧∧∧∧∧∧∧∧

In certain schools of reflexology, the fingertips are associated with the brain, and indeed fingertips that linger too long in a warm bath begin to pucker and crumple like the convolutions of the cerebrum.

In acupressure, the ring finger is associated with the ear
which provides an implied and cross-sensory pun
on "ring" as ornament and "ring" as tolling sound.

The pinkie, associated with delicacy of manners and an aversion to aggression, strikes the backspace key associated with typographical regret and second thoughts. The ring finger, associated with the delicately fraught duet of matrimony, strikes the number 2 as if to numerologically assure itself of its undertaking.

> Suitably, our index finger and our middle finger
> —partly devoted to pointing and profaning, respectively—
> collaborate on "scare quotes"
> that frequently tip over into "glare quotes."

▫▫▫▫▫▫▫▫▫▫▫▫▫▫▫▫▫▫▫▫▫▫▫▫▫▫▫▫▫▫

Two decades before he patented his V-for-victory hand signal, Winston Churchill injured one of his hands falling off a camel on a tour with Lawrence of Arabia. Two decades before his own less-convincing V-gesture, Richard Nixon used his index and middle fingers for accusation purposes during anti-Communist witch-hunts with Joe McCarthy.

> The fingers of the hand are rivers flowing
> from the delta of the palm
> and so the concerto-conducting index finger
> occasionally suffers from delusions of Danube
> and the middle finger from delusions
> of dammed-up Delaware.

If our ten fingers were directly aligned to the Ten Commandments, the following correspondences between Digit and Law would symbolically occur: the thumb would be expected to honor the Lord with its thumbs-up and the index finger would be especially forbidden from wearing an idol-bearing ring and the middle finger would need to stop taking the Lord's name in gestural vain.

The Roman salute revived by 20th century fascists
    possessed half of the gravitas,
        one-quarter of the empire,
            and none of the Stoicism.

≈∞≈∞≈∞≈∞≈∞≈∞≈∞≈∞≈∞≈∞

If safecrackers really do sandpaper
their fingertips for added sensitivity,
    ballerinas should consider walking on smoldering coals
        before dancing *The Firebird*
            or massaging their soles with lily-pads
                before dancing *Swan Lake*.

An Arabic legend tells us that God's finger fed Abraham by dispensing milk, honey, dates, water, and butter from different fingers like divine faucets, but doesn't tell us if the Deity's digits disputed over who among them would be demoted to water-boy.

Paul Celan claimed to see no difference between a poem and a handshake though presumably a haiku has more in common with a fist- bump than the *Iliad* does and a limerick is closer to a high-five than a sonnet is.

Will a species-wide mutation
    ever render our prehensile thumb posthensile
so exiled from its arboreal origins and twig-hunting for termites
    it is incapable of grasping
    and resigned to glad-handing and applauding its overlords?

«±«±«±«±«±«±±«±«±«±«±«±«±«±«±«

If our hand's palm is a figurative leaf,
    our arm is a branch
        and our torso a trunk
and whether we scatter mental acorns, dates, or coconuts
    is a matter of our disposition.

Generally, hands placed on hips are only assuming an attitude of imperial arrogance if the feet and the chin are willing to perform their supporting roles of widening and jutting, respectively. Similarly, two hands clasped together can be devout prayer or desperate exasperation or a blending of the two, depending on the degree of interlace and wrist-lock.

To our skin's tactile receptors, a "caress" must move at a particular speed across the skin to qualify as a caress (and not a protracted "nudge"), without moving so fast that it qualifies as a full-blown "flick."

According to Zen tradition,
the clenched fist cannot scoop from the running stream:
according to an amateur photographer tendency,
the finger that intrudes into the upper-left corner of a picture
cannot keep from making a cameo appearance.

Since the Tokugawa period in Japan, shiatsu massage has largely been a discipline of blind practitioners, whose fingers seem to develop their own visionary powers as if their tactile nerves shared common roots with the *bodhi* tree of Buddhist awakening.

When *schadenfreude* tries to wipe its hands on its apron
it leaves a telltale smear of Weimar sadism
and the Teutonic will-to-power:
When the speed-of-slap is the speed-of-caress cubed
the speed-of-catch is the square root of the speed-of-toss.

During the French Age of Enlightenment, Diderot believed that the hand's touch was vision minus color plus texture, rather than smell minus nostril-flare plus finger-stubbing, or taste minus gag reflex plus knuckle-cracking.

For reasons both manual and meaningful
"hand" as a verb
tends to be less lascivious and accusatory
and more generous and considerate
than "finger" as a verb.

❋:❋:❋:❋:❋:❋:❋:❋:❋:❋:❋:❋:❋:❋:❋:❋:❋:❋:

As the Stone Age turned into into the Iron Age, the overburdened hand gasped with a bit of relief, but when the Industrial Age turned into the Silicon Age, the hand blinked at its eerie absence of required actions.

In a hand-based logic
"tough" is always one consonant-swap away from "touch"
because "cares" is always a single sibilant short of "caress"
and "swipe" and "swap" are close phonetic kin
because "loan" can differ greatly from "lend."

Our cuticles are relics of our ancestor's claws and presumably precursors of our descendants' own eventual (and even less clawish) manual refinements. Modern paleontologists specializing in the human hand look for evidence of the shift from tree-climbing to tool-using, while themselves embodying the shift from rotary dial-turning to digital button-pushing.

Helen Keller listened to Caruso's vocal cords with her fingertips,
allowing tactility to convert his trills into drumrolls
on her hands' own tympani.

∧∧∧∧∧∧∧∧∧∧∧∧∧∧∧∧∧∧∧∧∧∧∧∧∧∧

In a contracture condition called the Viking's Disease, the fingers are always partially curved in toward the palm as if permanently clutching booty ransacked from a burning city. There is currently no Donation Disorder that bends the fingers in the opposite direction.

The hand used as a launching pad for a blown kiss
can convert into a forum for a forehead-slap
in the half-second it takes for flirtation to curdle into exasperation.

The Horned Hand, depending on the precise fingers involved, can signal a summons to the devil or a hex on an unfaithful wife. More benevolently, *el ojo en la mano*, "the eye in the hand," is both unblinking and unclenching in its vigilant gesture of protection.

The Philosopher's Hand tends to be gnarled and knotted
as if it had accumulated existential age-rings
gnostic knot-holes, cognitive calcium-spurs
and nominalist knuckle-folds with every act of cerebral grasping.

༄༄༄༄༄༄༄༄༄༄༄༄༄༄༄༄༄༄༄༄༄༄༄༄༄༄༄༄༄༄

No matter how quickly it is rotated, M.C. Escher's iconic *Drawing Hands* drawing remains a paradoxical cartwheel of a visual riddle, recursively hand-by-hand and lucratively hand-over-fist at once. That iconic photo of Picasso's bread hands, with a set of croissants giving the illusion of fingers gripping a table-edge, is an alimentary illusion and a manual metaphor at once.

A belly-pat and a belly-rub
   are the hands' twin poles of Satiation and Hunger
      just as an eye-rub and a knee-slap
   can be Disbelief manifesting at different anatomic latitudes.

The hand has more ligaments than the keys of a piano
 the strings of a banjo, and the tines of a kalimba combined:
  its ability to fan, knuckle-crack and wring its partner
   makes it a wind, percussion, and string instrument all at once.

What is the hand's equivalent of water tasting sweet after one eats an artichoke or white paper looking gray after one stares at sun-reflecting snow? Sandpaper feeling like a billiard ball after fondling barbed wire? Hands-in-pocket feeling like a grant of asylum after a too-long ovation?

++++++++++++++++++++++++++++

During the American Jazz Age, thumbs hooked into armpits meant careless confidence most emphatically when accompanied by a pair of argyle suspenders and a satin-banded straw boater.

 Our fingernails grow about as far
  as our major landmasses shift each year,
   suggesting a cosmic correspondence
    between our cuticles and our continents.

Anaxagoras claimed that "Man is the wisest of all animals because he has hands," in an effort to distance those hands from their topical relation to talons and paternal obligation to paws and heavy debt to hooves and family resemblance to fins.

Certain chess players have a hand-language
that inflects differently depending on the piece in question:
abruptly seizing a rook
but meditatively fondling a queen,
dramatically pinching a bishop
but swaying a king like a pendulum.

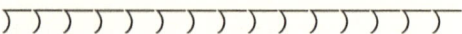

Why can "thumb" be used as a verb in a way that no other finger-noun really can? Is this a semantic segregation to underscore that digit's muscular isolation? And is our left pinkie prone to delusions of both Alpha and Omega because it strikes both "a" and "z" on a standard keyboard?

If a miser's hand can squeeze a dollar until the eagle screams
it can presumably also grip certain coins
until the pyramid's eye winces
and the obelisk of the Washington monument
explodes into a cloud of marble-dust.

Hand grenades, depending on their military intentions,
can be subdivided into white-knuckled fist grenades
fingers-crossed Hail Mary grenades
hands-free remote access grenades
and hand-over-fist military contractor grenades.

The more that a particular church congregation frowns on handclap-driven singing and hands-over-head testimony, the more likely its bake-sales are to be gluten-free.

☝☞☝☞☝☞☝☞☝☞☝☞☝☞☝☞☝

Manually, one can unpour by refilling, unwrap by removing
unmask by displaying, and unsettle by disturbing
but cannot unslap or unswing
unless one is willing to enter an alternative dimension
of actions anticipated but not acted-on.

In Chinese palmistry, the ring finger is "fire" and indeed its service as a ring-bearer immerses it in many a domestic inferno and ember-stirring divorce proceeding.

Sometimes a high-five is a form of hand-to-hand resuscitation and sometimes a fingersnap is a random syllable in a word too long to be easily remembered.

Give the hand its own ungendered pronoun
   and its sense of agency will be increased
      its sense of utility will feel less exploited,
   and its sense of duality will feel less duel-prone.

«±«±«±«±«±«±«±«±«±«±«±«±«±«±«±

Julian Huxley saw infants using their hands like monkeys do, and indeed if there were a manual phase of infant development to balance out the oral and anal phases, it would be a probe into our prehuman past.

A virtuoso hand-stander's excellence can be measured
   by her foot-fluttering gravity-defiance
      fullness of floor-grip
and tactile sense of terra firma erecting an inverted tower of Self.

Marc Chagall, painter of green violinists and floating horses, claimed that "The fingers must be educated, the thumb is born knowing," as if the thumb were the reptilian basal complex of the hand's brain, an atavistic hotline to the pineal command center.

Upright, bipedal walking was a moment of liberation for our hands
    that our feet lacked a vote in
  our spines paid the lobbying fee for
and said hands didn't fully applaud for several millennia.

****
****

If interlinking one's fingers behind one's head is the manual equivalent of crossing one's legs at the thigh, then conversely "flicking" rhymes with "kicking" for good reason.

    A so-called "manual" transmission
      actually entails several layers
  of go-between gearwork and engineered interface
between a driver's hands and a vehicle's responsiveness,
   though our overdriven id never fully admits
     to such ego-supporting enhancements.

Our thumb is much closer in size to our other fingers when compared to other primates because human hands have evolved less than a chimpanzee's hands in terms of digital differential, suggesting that humanity's labor-saving machinery has lessened our finger-based division-of-labor and democratized inter-digit relations to a large degree.

When a hand arches its "back" to form into a letter C
its so-called spine mimes a semaphoric citrus deficiency:
When a hand forms a letter V
its decisive index finger and renegade middle finger
have managed a cooperative ceasefire.

ꜫoʃoꜫoʃoꜫoʃoꜫoʃoꜫoʃoꜫoʃoꜫoʃ

Sometimes the trigger finger of an exterminator can't separate its tics from its twitches because its assigned prey has a hard time separating its spasms from its seizures.

If every item in a toolshed extends different aspects of the hand
then pliers are to Pull as tape measure is to Tally
but crowbar is to Caress as hacksaw is to Homogenize.

Isaac Asimov, with dozens of books to his credit, once blithely claimed that "Writing to me is simply thinking through my fingers." For others, however, writing is a knuckle-gnashing, cuticle-crunching, fingertip-furrowing anguish, a pen is a Spear of Mutiny, and a keyboard is a field of landmines.

Our eyes' pupils grow gradually smaller and smaller
 following peak size during pubescence:
subsequently, our hands develop a wider repertoire of gestures—from lyrical come-hithers to ludicrous finger-guns—
 to compensate for our eyes' seductive shortfall.

†††††††††††††††††††††††††††††

The lateral tripod grasp of a pencil resembles the support-stance of a field camera and underscores a writing implement's ability to record images and visions. The dynamic quadrupod grasp of a pencil more closely resembles a crouched cheetah and underscores a writing implement's function as a pursuer of semantic prey.

If a basketball team is indeed five fingers on a single hand,
 so is a well-tuned jazz quintet,
though drum-as-thumb and piano-as-pinkie and index-as-alto
 are all faulty and unflattering assumptions.

Seneca wrote that "there is no grace in a benefit that sticks to the fingers" but from within the confines of a Roman empire whose own sticky fingers scooped up unwilling tributes from the colonial pockets of over half of the Western world.

A fingersnap can break a silence in a fraction of an instant,
    but sat-upon hands can only restore said silence
        over a considerably longer duration
            because silence is more of an accumulation than a gap.

♯♯♯♯♯♯♯♯♯♯♯♯♯♯♯♯♯♯♯♯♯♯♯♯♯♯♯♯

Jerry Lee Lewis claims that his fingers have individual brains in them but doesn't specify if his thumb favors its medulla over its cerebrum
    or if his index finger favors its left hemisphere to its right
        or if his middle finger is prone to migraines
            when a spotlight is too searing.

In cartoon history, having less than five fingers per hand seems less of a problem for a white-gloved rodent than for a heroically caped city-saver, but Japanese cartoon characters of all species tend to have a five-digit hand to avoid resembling pinkie-sacrificing Yakuza gangsters.

Our very mobile index finger eventually causes a wrinkle to form between the head and heart lines on our palm, and so our large range of assertive, pointing gestures eventually widens the gap between mind and emotion from a palm-reader's perspective.

Some actors break the fourth wall with their hands,
while some make it ripple and reverberate
like a cobweb or a curtain.

::

Kant claimed that "the hand is the window onto the mind,"
but some people's hands are clearly more stained-glass
than luxury-liner porthole
and some are hung with half-stuck Venetian blinds
or encrusted with a permanent hangover's hoarfrost.

The fins that our transitional ancestors used to clamber onto dry land eventually became hands that occasionally paddle in our sleep, engaging in acts of neural nostalgia.

When Marcel Duchamp used a Rembrandt as an ironing board, he seemed to imply that the hands delight in blurring the line between Artwork and Utility and between what is Classic and what is Crease-Removing.

When lining up a round of fisticuffs
   the cracking of knuckles is a brief drumroll
      that prefigures its own rimshot
         and an operatic throat-clearing
           that overtures its own gasping encore.

«±

Whether to play a washboard vest with thimbles or with church-key bottle openers is as deep a manual, existential quandary in bayou Louisiana as whether to play slide guitar with a cigarette lighter or a AAA battery is on the Mississippi delta.

The hand that alternates directly between
   beard-scratching wistfulness and chin-cradling boredom
      needs a larger neutral gear in its manual transmission
   and a better-lubricated segue in its manual/cranial interface.

As a fallacy, "if you can move a finger, it's not broken" is lodged somewhere on the Liars' Litany in between "eating gelatin makes the fingernails stronger" and "cracking your knuckles causes arthritis."

"Hand" as an ever-adaptable transitive verb
is able to pair up with practically any preposition
so that "hand off" is within semantic reaching distance of
"hand to"
and "hand along" and "hand across"
can converge at particular angles.

∞∞∞∞∞∞∞∞∞∞∞∞∞∞∞∞∞∞∞∞∞

In studies, Italian hand-gestures tend to polish and sculpt
while Jewish gestures knit and pull threads,
suggesting that our senses of Statue and Scripture and Seamstress
all play a role in steering our hand-language.

Thoth--the ibis-headed Egyptian god of writing—possesses a name that is an acoustic but not a graphic palindrome, mirroring the hands' own palindroming of each other. In a more kinetic palindrome, our eyebrows are raised and lowered by the words others speak to us just as surely as our hands levitate and dunk the words we speak to others.

We could perhaps train our eyes to take turns blinking
to avoid being plunged into momentary intervals of darkness
but our hands may never learn to salute and clap at the same time
without being plunged into a permanent state of jingoism.

When warming one's hands at a military campfire, one's new-recruit pinkies tend to fall into beta-wave slumber before one's foot-soldier middle fingers forget their sentry-duty and one's brass-sporting index fingers surrender their unit command.

The "finger calendar" method reportedly allows one to reckon the day of the week for any date in history, but tends to dislocate a knuckle on the Gregorian reform and stub its cuticles on a Mayan sundial.

The number of pieces of popcorn per average grab
is determined by hunger, haste and hand-size
but slowed down by satiation, socialization, and slipperiness.

A Napoleon Bonaparte statue fulfilling its fabricated stereotype by tucking its hand into its cummerbund allows that hand to rummage through the Archives of the Untrue and the Hallways of the Historically Misleading.

The headwaiter able to balance a tray of martinis in one hand
and a tray of mezcal margaritas in the other
must have an evenly calibrated and bipartisan sense
of how the specific gravity of an olive differs from that of a worm.

※ ※ ※ ※ ※ ※ ※ ※ ※ ※ ※ ※

Biting one's fingernails comes in scallop, sawtooth, and serrated varieties that are the signatures for some of the primary species of human anxiety.

A human hand casts off skin-cells like a tree casts off leaves
in an unending anatomic autumn
and an eternal equinox of epidermal evacuation.

Salvador Dalí's painting *Apparatus and Hand* depicts a tumescently reddened hand protruding directly from a head as if to underscore the hand's service as the brain's non-optic periscope and the brain's service as the hand's duty-juggling command center.

In standard typewriting,
the left middle finger lays claims to the letters "d," "e," and "x"
as if staking out the third syllable of the word "ambidextrous"
and the right middle finger lays claim to the letters "k", "i," and "m"
as if seizing the initial monograms for "kinetic,"
"idiolect," and "manual" to compensate.

⦙⦙⦙⦙⦙⦙⦙⦙⦙⦙⦙⦙⦙⦙⦙⦙⦙⦙⦙⦙⦙⦙

Leon Theremin's eponymous instrument uses proximity sensors allowing the hand to weave melodies directly out of the air, as if strumming on soundwaves and finding octaves in an electron's orbitals.

A walking-cane allows a hand to be an additional foot
just as a brake pedal empowers a foot
to modulate a swerve decided on by a hand
while a hand-supported headstand
permits a foot to be a wavering salute
and a ladder allows our pedal steps
to levitate our manual grasp.

A bowling ball's fingerholes are not only invitations but sites of correspondence, designed by the hand to receive the hand's grip to extend the hand's aim, cradled by the hand to prepare the hand's thrust to attain the hand's objective, and wiped by the hand to clear off the hand's residues to serve the hand's persistence.

The French word for hand, spelled *main*,
can make that organ appear even more central than it already is
while the Welsh word for hand, *llaw*,
similarly makes it appear more commanding than it needs to be.

****

"Buddha's hand" is a variety of citrus fruit often referred to as a "lemon with fingers," almost all rind and no flesh and almost all fragrance and no flavor. Said fruit uses those fingers to tickle the nose rather than the taste buds and uses that rind to conceal its lack of pith rather than to protect it.

In one occult schema, the tip of the left pinkie is January
the space between pinkie and ring finger is February
and the ring finger is March
as if our hand were a vernal calendar
and our thumbs were the squat Stonehenge-pillars
on either side of a seasonal ritual.

The "hot hand" fallacy among gamblers imagines that a lucky roll of the dice or spin of the roulette wheel can communicate with the next roll or spin via some karmic current radiated by the fingers. The "cold hand" fallacy among writers imagines that a blank page is a tundra waiting to inflict its frostbite on the tip of a pencil.

The finger-cymbals of a flamenco dancer
and the chopsticks of a sushi-chef
if engaged in a fly-catching contest
would be engaging in percussion and predation at the same time.

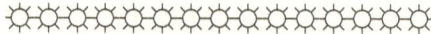

The Arabic word for hand—*yad*—eventually formed into an icon that became our precarious, vertical pronoun *I*. A Chinese character for the word *shou* ("hand") adorns its own vertical line with extra branches for better balance (手).

When the bullseye of a target is mentally imprinted
in the fingertips of a Zen archer's hand,
the words *aim* and *object*
and the prepositions *at* and *in*
switch places.

Some Hindu mudras, like the every-fingertip-pressed-against-its-counterpart-on-the-opposite-hand Hakini gesture, have been colonially hijacked by Bond villains and Wall Street bond-traders alike.

There is no widely recognized tactile or olfactory version
of clairvoyance or clairaudience because
our hands and our nose tend to be two-fisted, hard-nosed skeptics
compared to our illuminating, visionary pupils and spin-dizzy ears.

.:+:.:+:.:+:.:+:.:+:.:+:.:+:.:+:.:+:.:+:.:+:.:+:.

In an earlier phase of criminal history, certain bandits and burglars used a severed hand as a charm or talisman, as if an additional (though inoperative) hand added to their own avaricious extremities might unbalance the binary of Blame.

A steering-wheel becomes a swerving-wheel
when the hands lag behind the eyes:
a steering-wheel becomes a merging-wheel
when the hands and eyes interfuse and act as one.

When New York's Finger Lakes bunch into a tectonically knuckled fist-lake, the Aquatic End of Days is near. When a goodbye handshake's vigor depends on the altitude of its accompanying upper arm-grasp, the bicep has been turned into a barometer of bonhomie.

    Our fetal fingers are already folded and furrowed
        because our pre-existence in the amniotic sac
           imprints some of our anxieties
      and engraves some of our misgivings in advance.

^^^^^^^^^^^^^^^^^^^^^^^^^^^^

There are piano etudes that require wooden blocks to strike certain chords whose notes are too far apart to be straddled by mere human hands, but there is no novel so novel that it requires a similar maneuver on more than one typewriter at a time.

    If the callouses on the hand
      emulate the profession that inflected them,
          then the callouses of a roofer
              are more corrugated than those of a carpenter,
        those of a carpenter are more plank-like
           than the those of a mason,
              and those of a mason more gravelly
                than those of a pipefitter.

The hand raised to swear in a witness box is rarely allowed to raise a moistened forefinger to test the winds of Perjury or raise a pinkie before drinking from its own testimony's teacup. The hand sworn in on a closed Bible cannot direct its individual fingers to specific books of scripture in the middle of its oath.

The Latin word for hand, *manus*,
    is always a vowel-shift away from "minus"
despite the additive and avaricious elements of the grasping hand.

▫▫▫▫▫▫▫▫▫▫▫▫▫▫▫▫▫▫▫▫▫▫▫▫▫▫▫▫▫▫

Did the silent "l" in "palm" go to the same pronunciation purgatory as the "w" in "wrist" or to the same elision limbo as the first "k" in "knuckle"? If "white-knuckled" means stricken with a paralyzing fear, what knuckle-color is emblematic of over-confidence and a willingness to plunge into Worry's wet cement?

When the hand engages in air-quotes
to avoid accusations of anti-irony
its inverted commas undermine its own claims
and only underscore its own evasion of engagement.

In Vedic tradition, the henna-leaf tattooing of hands
follows natural nerve-meridians
to illustrate and underscore the rays of our Inner Sun
as well as the tributaries and deltas of our Inner River
and the stellar configurations of our Inner Galaxy.

The hands that flatten out the wrinkles in one's skirt when sitting down to an interview are the same hands that will crumple up error-stricken documents once that interview has been passed.

≈∞≈∞≈∞≈∞≈∞≈∞≈∞≈∞≈∞≈∞≈∞

Heidegger referred to "an abyss of essence" separating the human hand from claws and paws and talons, but this abyss has neurological rope-bridges and spanner-platforms that make the crossing of that abyss easier at moments of appetite and ill temper.

The veins and arteries of the wrist and hand
and their different blood-colors
are the lenses on the Incoming/Outgoing
traffic-signal of our metabolism,
glowing blue when in need of a pit-stop
at the oxygen pump
and pink when fueled to capacity
and ready to resume their road trip.

Presumably the hand-languages of 100-decibel drill-workers and vow-of-silence monks differ in terms of beer-agitated declaratives as well as signs of wine-warmed benediction.

The heel of the hand operates more often like the keel of a boat
or the wheel of a cog
than the heel of the foot
which is itself a kneel-initiator and a reel-stabilizer
when the seal of stable posture has been unpeeled.

«±«±«±«±«±«±«±±«±«±«±«±«±«±«±«±«±«

No species of animal known to evolutionary science possesses an odd number of hands, though Charles Darwin himself occasionally used his mouth as a third hand when he was collecting beetles in the field and needed one of his storage-hands freed up to grasp an additional specimen.

When removing one's eyeglasses in disbelief
use a lateral sweep to signal "rage"
an underhand grip to mean "awe"
and an overhead clasp to indicate "slow-motion disdain."

The co-creator of Batman was Bill Finger and one of the co-animators of Snow White was David Hand, but no one by the surname of Fist has yet volunteered to work on the hyperviolence of a Japanese manga.

Since fingernails and hairs are both forms of modified skin
a manicurist can impersonate a grinding-stone
for an epidermis-gone-bladelike
and a barber can impersonate a scythe at work
on a field of epidermis-gone-weedlike.

ʃʃ

The rivalry between a person's two hands can only be compared to the competition between siblings at the risk of turning the fingers into a Freudian family romance and the palms into half-willing ambassadors during moments of reluctant applause.

The *mano secreto* or esoteric hand-doctrine of conga players encourages the hand to flutter like a Havana diving-board
sway like a Santiago palm-frond
and cup like a Fort Lauderdale salad-bowl.

In some alternate dimension of recuperative art history, Venus de Milo's missing hands are scratching the missing nose of the Sphinx, chin-cradling Winged Victory's headless bust, and caressing and consoling Van Gogh's ear.

The sound of one mummified monkey's paw clapping
   is a conundrum sounding on a Zen drumskin
   and a paradox made possible by a taxidermist
echoing where the prayer hall and the primate house intersect.

❀:❀:❀:❀:❀:❀:❀:❀:❀:❀:❀:❀:❀:❀:❀:❀:❀:❀:

If a typewriter were as touch-sensitive as a piano, one could modulate nouns and bend vowels and trill one's ellipses. If one's handwriting features loops large enough to lasso ideas, then its crossbars can afford to be miniature diving boards leading off into the white space of further speculation.

If Hercules' twelve classical labors were made virtual
   in today's era of scrolling-and-swiping technology
   his callouses would all cluster protectively at his thumbs
and an ergonomic office chair would slide under each ordeal.

When buried in the rotating clay on a potter's wheel
      the fingers learn to be done-to even while doing
      and to revel in the blur between active and passive:
When the hands flutter in cowardice
but the feet insist on planting heroically,
      the torso twists in a crosswind of self-contradiction
    and visceral veto-power.

Humans blink away 24 minutes of every day but tend to finger-snap and hand-clap away just a few seconds unless we are especially impatient or ovation-prone.

^^^^^^^^^^^^^^^^^^^^^^^^^^^^

In Dr. Strangelove Alien Hand Syndrome, the hand engages in its own fascist salutes against its owner's "will." A Dr. Frankenstein version of this syndrome would struggle against the desire to animate corpses with lightning bolts as surely as a Dr. Jekyll version would struggle against too-quick costume changes.

The legend that claims that caviar fishermen
    are born with black fingernails
      suggests that Character is carved out by Cuticle
        and that Keratin can counsel a Caspian career.

A map of North America painted on a hand has the option of using the peninsula of a pinkie as a Florida or a Baja California depending on the artist's attitude toward relative humidity and whether or not the palmar or dorsal side of the hand is the better canvas.

If a bald man can run his hand through the memory of his hair
    a retired Hall of Fame boxer
can use his aging palms to envy and applaud
    his own ungloved and unfisted hands' fading virtuosity
    and a cane to supplement and punctuate
his once-dazzling footwork.

࿇࿇࿇࿇࿇࿇࿇࿇࿇࿇࿇࿇࿇࿇࿇࿇࿇࿇࿇࿇࿇࿇࿇࿇࿇࿇࿇࿇

In Chinese palmistry, the forefinger is associated with Water
    and is indeed a prow scudding
        through the fractal foam of decision-making
            when it taps impatiently on a desktop
    and a mainsail when its pointing
is powered by the wind of Willfulness.

Since we traditionally knock three times on a door to symbolize Faith, Hope, and Charity, perhaps any additional knocks should be heard as transgressions against those very virtues, and as the percussion-strikes of Apostasy, Pessimism, and Callousness.

When Chinese New Year coincides with Valentine's Day, the giving hand and embracing arm are pulled between fireworks and floral arrangements, dragon parades and dark chocolates, and paper lanterns and passion's dimmed lighting.

The fingernails are also a window on the spirit:
just as blue in the cuticles can indicate a lack of oxygen in the lungs
    and white in the nail-beds can indicate anemia
        bitemarks along the outer lunula
            can indicate angst or ennui on an eating-spree.

++++++++++++++++++++++++++++

The classical Greek word for "thumb" translates to "another hand," perhaps because the thumb's range of services is nearly as wide and eclectic as the rest of the fingers combined and because its placement suggests a secession from the mainland of the other digits.

Birds have magnetite in their heads to point them north
    and fireflies have luciferase to provide bioluminescence
    but the human hand has yet to develop an enzyme
    that would make for more legible prescriptions
    or impossible-to-forge autographs.

A certain kind of archer's hand learns to see a target's concentric circles as a ripple caused by a stone yet to be dropped and to hear the pulling-back of the bow as the gentle uprooting of a plant that has become too firmly embedded to grow.

Sometime the notches on the pistol-grip of a Wild West gunman
    resembled the bars of a waiting jail-cell
      or the steps of the ladder leading to the gallows,
        especially if his instep-to-stirrup coordination
couldn't keep pace with his hand-to-holster coordination.

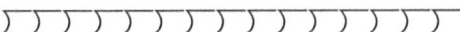

Since Elvis Presley's lascivious gyrations were shot by camera-crews from the waist up, maybe Al Jolson's dance, with its lewdly wagging hands, should have been shot from the elbows in.

From a manual perspective:
    New Jersey being shaped like an old woman sewing
  influenced Michigan being shaped like a single lost mitten
about as much as Florida's resemblance to a finger pressed to a page
    influenced Colorado being shaped like an unopened book.

The Egyptian Ka, or vital spirit-force, is often depicted as a sun whose rays end in human hands. There is no preserved record of any pharaoh fearing the day when those hands would close vengefully into solar-flare fists or swing punitively into solar-wind slaps.

In keeping with the hands' basic dualism
there is rarely a nest for the Dove of Peace and the Hawk of War
to realize their nuptials
at the crotch of a V-for-Victory hand-gesture.

࿇࿇࿇࿇࿇࿇࿇࿇࿇࿇࿇

The maternal "hand that rocks the cradle" and the anarchist "hand that cradles a rock" can graze past each other's fingertips and half-grasp each other's wrists without ever achieving the kind of solid consensus that comes from a fully committed handclap.

When a hand wants to fool a motion-sensor
into believing that it is only a passing butterfly
it prepares by performing cross-species calisthenics
in the form of wing-flaps and petal-landings.

The master god of the Mesoamerican Nahuas was known by a name that means "hand," and perhaps coincidentally the Nahuas measured a man's height from his feet to however far overhead his hand would reach, as if to gauge a man's full stature by how close to the god-hosting heavens his hand could extend.

Our two hands collaborate on a deftly executed Heimlich maneuver
(one clasping and covering the folded-up fist of the other)
in a gesture that vaguely resembles the spooning of sleeping lovers
in an effort to rescue a choking victim from an endless sleep
brought on by an errant feeding-spoon.

«±«±«±«±«±«±«±«±«±«±«±«±«±«±«±

The Mayans' master sky-god was also known by a name that means "hand," and perhaps coincidentally, the echoes in a particular Mayan pyramid chirp like a heaven-seeking bird if one claps one's hands while standing inside of it.

A jazz drummer's traditional grip is a rotating mismatch
of underhand and overhand,
supine for the snare and prone for the pulse
and then upside-out for an accent
and downside-in for a diddley-beat
in a self-propelled mandala
orbiting its own sense of meter.

Presumably a pianist's hand insurance features different sub-clauses and exemptions than a brain surgeon's because atonal dissonance is not a form of aggravated malpractice and a sour note is not a severed nerve.

When the fingers impersonate a team of ten tongues
    gluttony becomes a matter of grabbing
        fasting is made possible by a closed fist
and an empty stomach is best impersonated with an open hand.

****
****

By now, Adam Smith's invisible hand is an economic poltergeist haunting the moss-hung mansion of global capitalism just as surely as a raised fist with hammer and sickle is a disillusioned specter roaming the poster-plastered hallways of regional communism.

A human infant crawls in a "plantigrade" manner
rather than knuckle-walking like its cousins the apes
as if sharpening the whorls of its fingerprints
on the whirl of the planet's rotation
and temporarily training its palms
to recognize the lay of the land its feet will soon tread alone.

The blind tend to use hand gestures even when speaking among themselves, demonstrating that these gestures operate not only as illustrators and accents but as engines and invigorators.

The hand that tries to forcibly smash a case of writer's block
    back into its component pebbles
occasionally finds said block turning into a 20-story
        Babylonian ziggurat
made of fiercely polished marble
    or an East-West dividing wall
        garlanded with barbed wire and gun-turrets.

☙◦❧◦☙◦❧◦☙◦❧◦☙◦❧◦☙◦❧◦☙◦❧◦☙◦❧◦

The so-called hang-loose hand gesture popular among Hawaiian surfers narrowly avoids being the horned-hand cuckold gesture popular among Italians by moving its pivot-point one digit over, from the index finger to the thumb. Frequently, the distance between a blessing and a hex is a mere fraction of a finger.

According to body-language studies,
    there is an implied box in front of one's torso
that tends to contain the most effective hand gestures
       though this box can be folded in half by shyness
          enlarged by megalomania
             or corrugated by a vodka hangover.

In Colette's short story "The Hand," a newlywed wife gazes into the wild pasture of her sleeping husband's hairy hand and follows its veins and sinews backward into the open savannah and arboreal canopies of our primate prehistory.

If crossed fingers could indeed wipe away an act of perjury
crossed legs could kick away a charge of lewd behavior
and crossed arms could bear-hug away an accusation of harassment.

††††††††††††††††††††††††††††††

The artist whose bare-handed medium is the smoke-sculpture learns to stride along the barrier that separates the statuesque from the ephemeral and the monumental from the transient. The magician whose hand can hurl playing cards and plant them into the outer skin of a watermelon learns the secret of a rind-lodged royal flush.

So-called Hand-of-God clouds form every once in a while,
though whether they are perceived as thunder-clutching
or bouquet-bearing or rain-strewing
depends on the belief-systems of the regions they hover above.

The ancient Greeks buried the offending hand of a suicide in its own separate grave, whether or not the mode of self-nullifying was manual or not. This form of anatomic scapegoating would presumably allow the feet of a bridge-jumper and the gullet of a poison-swallower to avoid their portion of mortal blame in a pre-classical tragedy.

The Fibonacci spiral has been referred to as "God's fingerprint"
    as if a forensics team of sacred geometers
        had detected manual evidence of it
    coiled divinely at the crime-scene of our cosmos' origin.

###############################

The pinkie is the ear finger in certain religions, used to plug the ear while chanting or petitioning. Since chanting is an attempted message to the gods, it is suitable that Mercury (quicksilver courier to the other-world) is the patron of the pinkie.

In a fully animistic universe
    the handprints of a lecherous Hollywood mogul
        if cast into wet cement
           would begin grasping at the ankles and calves
                of passersby upon drying.

If there is a Picasso of manicurists, her rose and blue phases will be tolerated but her Cubist period will mean a loss of income. If some twelve-handed god is required to juggle the moons of a year, then the autumn equinox is a manual as well as an annual labor.

    A round of prayer-beads can be
      a self-granted victory lap for the hands
        a circling of mental buzzards over moral carrion
          or a circular surveillance on the lookout for a loophole
    depending on one's motive for meditation.

::

When finger-painting, an overeager child's forearms can also be enlisted to smear a waterfall or smudge chimney-smoke across a canvas. Such a child has a more polymorphous sense of the Manual, with hands that begin at the elbow instead of merely at the wrist.

    The lowest Roman numerals represent human fingers
    though II can't cross those fingers
    any more than I can crack its knuckle
    or III can form into a fist.

    The contours of our fingerprints
        feature so-called "tents" and "arches"
allowing them to resemble the dwellings of a
    nomadic Mongol horde
        as well as the neoclassical architecture
    of the city that horde is about to invade.

    The Arabic salaam and the Catholic sign of the cross are both multi-stage hand gestures but differ in their attitudes toward fingers-to-forehead pivoting and the directional relations between the head and the heart.

∞∞∞∞∞∞∞∞∞∞∞∞∞∞∞∞∞∞∞∞

    A French claque is a team of professional applauders who are literal hands-for-hire, a sort of happily inverted equivalent to those mercenary mourners paid to wail and moan in the front row at Chinese funerals.

    Presumably, a centipede with hands in place of feet
        would be capable
        of a circuitous round of applause
            an algebraically complicated salute
            and a self-contained baton relay.

Gripping a steering-wheel with one's hands at noon and dusk
or at Genesis and Revelation, or at nucleus and tangent
instead of the conventionally prescribed ten and two
makes for more dramatic turns but less steady straightaways.

In his reputed last words, Alexander the Great requested his empty hands be left dangling out of his coffin to demonstrate our inability to transport our possessions across the transom of mortality, even though Alexander's sword-bearing, troop-guiding hands were the grandest evidence for our ability to gather possessions within the mortal sphere.

If a particular Bach fugue required a twelve-fingered organist or a certain Stravinsky ballet were scored for four-footed dancers, they would also operate as indirect critiques of the limits of our mammalian evolution.

According to an alternative palmistry
sometimes a love-line leaves the palm of a hand
and wraps around the wrist like a barbed-wire bracelet
subliminally reinforcing the "lock" in "wedlock"
and the "house-bound" root of the word "husband."

As humanity gradually stood upright
and half of its former feet became hands,
the seeds of the ovation and the slingshot
and the cartwheel were all planted in non-numerical order.

Does "clap" rhyme with "slap" and "paw" with "claw" for more direct reasons than "wrist" rhymes with "fist" but in parallel to "bunch" rhyming with "punch"?

Ж Ж Ж Ж Ж Ж Ж Ж Ж Ж Ж

The hands know that the kind of meat a burglar lays down to distract a watchdog depends on the breed of dog and the item being burgled, just as the feet know that the best getaway path depends on the items being hauled as well as the floor-surface being traversed.

The Spanish word *mano* contains the English word "man" and indeed the hand is a homunculus, a miniature "me" able to convert into its own puppet.

The lag-time between an initiating wave of greeting and a return wave of acknowledgement is often protracted or accelerated by the forces of company rank, gross income, and relative caffeination.

In terms of prosthetic architecture
    if a glove compartment is a closet for the hand
      a hatband can serve as a hand's attic
      a tie-clip as its storm window
          and a cargo pocket as its root-cellar.

                    ᛞᛞᛞᛞᛞᛞᛞᛞᛞᛞᛞᛞᛞᛞᛞᛞᛞᛞᛞᛞ

Reach down deep enough into a foot-locker full of war memorabilia and your hand will come out coated in the toxic residue of belligerence, the vintage patina of courage, and rust-particles from an inactive chain of command.

On sabbath-days when the hand is forbidden
from touching appliances
    a radio turned on by a power-surge
        a blender switched on by a wagging tail
    or a videocamera turned on by an errant daydream
        are all formidable foes.

George Steiner claims that an intellectual is someone who always reads with a pencil in hand—presumably to jot down ideas inspired by the ideas of others but also to drum-roll during moments of suspense and cymbal-splash at moments of climax.

Crossing one's index and middle fingers behind one's back
may place a footnote under a promise
but crossing one's pinkie over one's ring finger
cannot marginalize one's degree of matrimony.

****

In terms of manual-sartorial correspondence, perhaps the decibel limit for an acceptable golf clap should be determined in part by the loudness of the plaid pants sported by the golfers at the tournament in question.

We measure a horse's height in human hands
  but would never submit to measuring human height in hooves
because of equal parts hominid hubris and anti-equine arrogance

In a game of American football, the hands have a much larger repertoire of functions than the feet. In handball, the feet skid sideways so much they leave a spoor resembling a scrambled egg. In paddleball, the hands are supplemented with a slap-on-a-stem. In raquetball, the hands are supplemented with a ricochet-on-a-rocket-launcher.

The fingers can form a louvred Venetian blindfold
    whenever shame or shock requires us
        to look away in terror and gaze in horror at the same time.

An old phonebook advertisement encouraged our fingers to walk across the pages of our local directory, but stopped short of telling them to treat an ellipsis like a hopscotch board or to dance in circles around the maypole of an exclamation point.

A looser handshake is generally preferred
    among many Islamists and Asians,
        who regard the intensity of the European grip
            as a vise and a vice
                and a manual microcosm of Manifest Destiny.

The Germanic word *Woedenspanne* refers to the space between the thumb and the index finger, and considering that space's wide, overtaxed range of functions, it is fitting that it is named for Woden, the eclectically employed god of healing and the gallows, dice-throwing and royalty, sorcery and the alphabet.

    Instead of merely giving a generic hand in marriage,
        the noncommittal give their tentative pinkie
            the resentful give their steel-clad fist
                and the claustrophobic give their pried-open palm.

Among the deaf, so-called "spirit fingers" are a silent version of applause, in which wiggling takes the place of clapping. If such an ovation included a gestural equivalent of the wolf-whistle or heckling, all eyes would be on the middle finger to provide such services.

    Our hand-posture atrophies
        toward a more ape-like carriage as we age,
            moving both forward toward an embrace of the grave
    and backward toward a low-five of our
        prehuman primate history.

The Navajo contend that a Spirit Wind radiates from our fingerprints, envisioning our soul as capable of spinning a cyclone from the corrugated prairie of our epidermis. From a microbe's perspective, a rotary phone-dial causes a small-scale tornado every time a human hand races to reach a radio dedication line.

Hand-tools released the teeth from some of their burdens
with the corkscrew playing surrogate for the canines
and the mallet standing in for the molars
and the ice-pick substituting for the incisors.

^^^^^^^^^^^^^^^^^^^^^^^^^^^^

If our five fingers were forced to correspond to English's five main vowels, presumably more of our digits would place sealed bids on the egoistic *i* than the grunt-working *u*. Cracking one's knuckles says "ready" in the vocabulary of Preparation but says "idle" in the vocabulary of Distraction.

If our toeprints are as unique as fingerprints
    the sands of our beaches are composed of strata upon strata
        of spoor-sentences, step-letters
            and half-erased signatures.

Our hand's cuticles can only grow so long before they begin to curl inward like bamboo wrapping itself around a jeep-axle or squid-tentacles wrapping around a sunken ship's hull.

When a senior citizen's hands ache at the onset of a tropical storm
either rheumatism is a barometer using blood as its mercury
or arthritis is a weather balloon using blood as its helium.

◻◻◻◻◻◻◻◻◻◻◻◻◻◻◻◻◻◻◻◻◻◻◻◻◻◻◻◻◻◻

Forming a window with one's fingers, one calls attention
to the outer limits of one's perspective
as well as the lace-curtains of one's sentimentality
and the accumulated grime of one's biases.

Sometimes clapping hands are a drugstore cowboy and a cigar-store Indian agreeing on a border tax. Sometimes a musical composition based on a plummeting stock market requires a cellist's hands to quake and tremor like an inverse-floater zero-coupon bond set ablaze by a fever in someone's commodity holdings.

Sometimes we clasp a lover's hand as if it were an item of carnal contraband to be smuggled across the state line of sexual arousal, sometimes we grasp a potential foe's hand as if a handshake's ability to handcuff weren't so noticeable.

Fordism, as an approach to mass manufacture
   measures workers by how many productive manual motions
      they can perform in a given time-frame:
  reducing us to wallops per week, downstrokes per day
elbow-flexes per hour, moldings per minute
     and screw-turns per second.

≈∞≈∞≈∞≈∞≈∞≈∞≈∞≈∞≈∞≈∞

If a United Nations Hand-Salute existed, it would require a triple-jointed wrist to perform it, a polylingual tongue to describe it, and a security detail the size of Swiss banking-firm to neutralize and wrestle its more ominously outdated gestures to the ground.

A hand extended out of a car window to feel for rain
  is a tactile empiricist in terms of evidence
     and a self-informing skeptic in terms of climate impact
        a democratic anti-essentialist in terms of droplets
  and a utilitarian agnostic in terms of the need for an umbrella.

A Samuel Beckett stage direction involves switching from grasping one's nose between the right forefinger and thumb to that same grasp performed by the left forefinger and thumb, a gesture-shift that takes on monumental importance when performed on a minimalist stage but unclear insignificance when performed at an outdoor festival.

If Napoleon's hand tucked inside of his vest
was engaging in a dark-funded diplomatic summit
conference with itself
    Mussolini's hand tilted toward the heavens
was attempting to launch an unreciprocated
embrace of the Olympians.

«±«±«±«±«±«±«±±«±«±«±«±«±«±«±«±«

The hand that composes a symphony and the hand that conducts it often find themselves in a thumb-wrestling match at that piece's crescendos and in bland golf-clap agreement at its adagio.

Manually, a sense of camaraderie with the objects we handle
can emphasize the "pal" in "palpable"
underscore the "kin" in "kinetic"
and force a slant-rhyme between "tribal" and "tactile."

The Sufi dervish points downward with his left hand and supplicates upward with his right, using his hands as end-points on a rotating axis of worship as spiral as a serpent's staircase en route to skin-shedding salvation.

Our handwriting tends to smear its own statements
      and smudge its own signature
whenever it feels the twin pressures of Alias and Alibi
      upon its pen-grip's every pivot.

Our hands can wink
(in conspiratorially cross-species recognition)
to a porpoise's fin and an eagle's wing
with more confidence than our feet can wink
to a manatee's fluke or an amoeba's pseudopod.

Lao Tzu tells us the superior man makes his weak and weaponless left hand the "place of honor," clearly valuing the so-called "sinister" hand over the sword-wielder and the so-called "gauche" hand over the grenade-launcher.

Hand-milked cows give richer milk than machine-milked cows, only partially because the spigots of a cow's udders mirror the fingers of its human milker.

The ten fingers are also the ten Divine Attributes
on the human hand's Tree of Knowledge
only occasionally prone to digital Dutch Elm disease
or a root-rot of the reflexes.

❋:❋:❋:❋:❋:❋:❋:❋:❋:❋:❋:❋:❋:❋:❋:❋:❋:❋:❋:

In a French manicure, a chevron is superimposed on the natural "smile line" of a cuticle. This chevron differs from the one bestowed on French military generals both in size, internal angle, and willingness to engage in fisticuffs.

"Rasp" seems to reside inside of "grasp"
so that our grip has enough grain and roughage:
"rip" seems to reside inside of "grip"
to remind us of the violence our hands are capable of.

Considering what "prehensile" means,
 "posthensile" would mean "no longer interested in grasping"
  or "beyond the need to clutch"
 and would perhaps best be applied to Buddhist monks
  who have transcended the need for
  even the humblest of possessions.

The Dharmachakra mudra depicts the Buddha's thumb and forefinger joined together in a serene circle, but this same gesture can be an obscene orifice mimicry in certain parts of the world where the Cross managed to fend off the Bodhi Tree and prayer prevailed over meditation.

༄༄༄༄༄༄༄༄༄༄༄༄༄༄༄༄༄༄༄༄༄༄༄༄༄༄༄༄༄

The hand models used in watch catalogues
 need to be especially alert
  to Time's grasping, fumbling impact on their extremities
 just as foot models need to be alert
  to the onward, toe-stubbing march of the years.

The impulsive pinkie that doesn't wait for its more-rational index finger's ink to dry will smear that ink into a smudge that resembles a plume of smoke, as if impersonating a locomotive from its place in the hand's caboose.

Albrecht Dürer's etching *Praying Hands* appears on Andy Warhol's Catholic tombstone, though M.C. Escher's anatomically palindromic *Drawing Hands* and its spiral of hands-drawing-hands-drawing-hands has yet to appear on the mausoleum of any well-known believers in reincarnation.

When a pinkie-and-pointer-extended hand
    pantomimes the horns of a half-moon
        it subdivides its ability to mimic a full-moon fist
and compromises its ability to pantomime a solar eclipse.

++++++++++++++++++++++++++++++

There are forms of deep-tissue massage based on principles of grammar and semantics, in which a masseur's hands work on the tissues like texts, turning a knotted full-stop into a limber comma and a misspelled muscle-cramp into a more more articulate flexor.

Since a handshake is a literal currency
    passing one person's voltage into another's waiting dynamo
        along two digital directions in a single sweep
    every manual greeting is a mobile charging-dock
        and a meter-reader at once.

Working as a manual laborer generally precludes cultivating long fingernails, though some typists and data processors manage to smuggle in a long pinkie-cuticle in defiance of the merciless auto-manicure of a keyboard's cuticle-crunching.

If we maintained one hand for writing
and one hand for erasing
our sense of self-segregation would be more underscored
and our ability to self-censor would be nearly simultaneous.

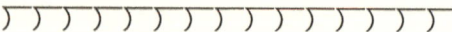

The last audience member to stop applauding and the last audience member to begin laughing are only the same person in special cases of ear-to-hand discoordination.

Keeping one's hands one "step" ahead of one's accusers
    sometimes requires an alibi
        as precarious as a headstand
      or an alias
    as nimble as a cartwheel.

Descartes believed that our sensual pleasures were the bonding agents that kept our souls and bodies firmly connected: of the manual pleasures of squeezing, stroking, and probing, which is the staple, which is the duct tape, and which is the rubber cement?

To update a Zen koan:
   the sound of one finger snapping
      is sometimes a pint of silence
         being ladled into a gallon of soundproofing.

♪♪♪♪♪♪♪♪♪♪

Drumming one's fingers on a department store countertop
is not necessarily more commerce-driven
than drumming one's fingers on a volunteer sign-in clipboard unless that drumming is punctuated
by revenue rimshots and price-adjusted press-rolls.

Handing a highway patrolman your license with your drink-raising hand and your registration with your resisting-arrest hand is a surefire recipe for manacles.

Applause is referred to collectively as "a hand," but a stampede is never referred to singularly as "a foot," despite a round of applause's clear kinship with a herd's thundering hoofbeats.

The feet "take" steps but "make" tracks
    where the hands "make" gestures but "take" hold,
        in a kind of criss-cross of anatomic Intake and Output.

****
****

The sweat on a palm pools into finger lakes only after the glacier of a whole-body grimace has survived a high-anxiety Ice Age. Blood pools and bulges in our hands when they are held below our heart but suitably flattens and thins in shame when engaged in an above-the-heart fascist salute.

Sometimes our middle finger is a flickering neon bulb
    in a roadside motel's No Vacancy sign
        sometimes it is the last smoldering ember in an act of arson
        and sometimes it is an outmoded antennae receiving signals
            it hasn't yet learned to digitally bypass.

Those nerve protocols that allow the fingertips to communicate directly with the wrist's jerk reflex without notifying the brain or forearm save the body a great deal of bureaucratic blue-blood tape and inter-office endocrine traffic.

If hand-watchers compiled their own field guide
the way that bird-watchers do
that book would contain species
like the Ruby-Throated Gearshift Grabber
and the Blue-Crested Baton Wielder.

༃ʃoʃ༃ʃoʃ༃ʃoʃ༃ʃoʃ༃ʃoʃ༃ʃoʃ༃ʃoʃ༃ʃoʃ

After an instantly regretted haircut
unnerved hands spend much time reshaping
what has been misshapen,
using the heel as an alternative comb
and saliva as a jerry-rigged gel
and fingers as counter-scissors.

If Gaston Bachelard is correct and we remember certain staircases from the top step down and others from the bottom step up, how vivid would a handrail have to be to be remembered from its middle out in both directions at once?

Just as a drop of ink dissipated into a pool of water is entropically unlikely to re-concentrate into a drop again, the pages of a diary torn up by trembling hands in a fit of sexual rage are unlikely to reassemble into a pre-lumber-mill stretch of virgin forest.

In terms of gesture-blurring, "chuckle" and "snort"
are permitted to blend into "chortle,"
but "grab" and "fondle" should be discouraged
from blending into "grandle."

†††††††††††††††††††††††††††††††

The hand that wishes to be placed on a blank journal during an oath of an office is already admitting to a crime of omission. The hand that engages in a piledriver of a pat on the back causes its recipient's cufflinks to clank and clatter like a discordant lapse in etiquette's percussion section.

In the etheric constellation of our astral dream-body
our hands are pulsing balls of gas preparing to supernova
into new gestures and actions
greed-and-gravity sinkholes
lurking behind an event horizon of avarice
and asteroids of gesture-emission
orbiting an axis of spinal alignment.

In the tai-chi motion "cloud hands"
  the extremities gently emulate the hydrologic cycle
    from hip-level ocean
      to shoulder-level vapors
  before breaking into a soft-falling rain of perspiration.

The novelist's hand that places a semicolon inside a piece of quoted dialogue has given a fictional character a sense of coordination and conjunction that would ordinarily deflate a speech-bubble.

♯♯♯♯♯♯♯♯♯♯♯♯♯♯♯♯♯♯♯♯♯♯♯♯♯♯♯♯

Montaigne once wrote a single sentence that lists 45 verbs that the hand is capable of: nine verbs for every finger that contributed to the sentence and half a verb for every degree in the angle our elbow adopts at the onset of arm-wrestling.

A film director directs not only his actors
but his audience's eyes—
a director of pornography
directs his audience's hands and loins as well.

In the nomenclature of voluntary plummeting, when sport-diving from a high board, one's hands serve as blade-tips for the body's dagger, but when free-diving from a tropical cliffside, one's hands are the head of the body's hammer. In the nomenclature of pirouetting, one's hands play Earth and Moon to the solar plexus or locale and antipode to the abdominal core or mutually pursuing asteroids around the stellar axis of the spine.

The Italian gesture of the pursed hand
    dispenses a coinage of over-spilling emotion
        and mints a hard currency of emphasis and exclamation
            spending overdrafts of *buono* and *bello*
                during times of gestural inflation.

::

In some manual dimension of the aphorism, the old proverb "Every honest miller has a thumb of gold" waits to be joined by "Every fugitive-from-justice hitchhiker has a thumb of rain-tarnished brass" and "Every retired gardener has a thumb of moldering compost."

The Indo-European word-nubbin *gr-*
    goes lewd in *grope*
        and desperate in *grasp*
            and resistant in *grapple*
to prove its versatility as a hand-assisting consonant cluster.

If pointing a finger at the moon results in a wooden finger (as warned in an old superstition), then aiming a rocket at the cosmos should petrify the Florida panhandle and aiming a cathedral at a constellation should render a scripture into sawdust.

    The so-called "hand" on the nuclear button
is made to feel more handlike
        by the atavistic allusions of missile-names:
    the BGM109 Tomahawk,
        the AGM-84 Harpoon,
    and the FGM-14 Javelin.

∞∞∞∞∞∞∞∞∞∞∞∞∞∞∞∞∞∞∞∞

    Manuals on Zen archery warn not to allow the bow-releasing hand to pop open like a ripe fruit-skin, presumably favoring the gradual opening of an ascetic lotus to the ardent gush of a pomegranate's pulp and the gentle un-petaling of the chrysanthemum to the quick snap of a yuzu's rind.

    A closed-but-not-yet-cleaned tavern provides plenty of evidence—torn napkins, twisted match-sticks, folded coasters—
    of all of the miniature violence the hands perform
        while lips are speaking the language of seduction.

Humankind's hand-tools emulate other animals' appendages:
a claw hammer like a falcon's nut-prying talon
pliers like a branch-grasping lemur's pincer-grip
and a snow-shovel like a manatee's fluke.

Many a science fiction story deals with an enchanted typewriter able to produce text without the aid of human hands, playing into our anxieties about word-processing turning into word-parthenogenesis in a post-manual world.

The Cherokee medicine man who makes an uncoiling hand-motion over a snakebite to undo its venom will need to add some wave-like gestures to his repertoire when global warming brings shark-bites into the hinterlands of Oklahoma.

Door-knobs, coin-slots, and elevator buttons
not only anticipate but reflect the hand,
    just as a turnstile reflects the hips
        and a stairway refracts the feet
           and an entry-way projects head-ducking.

A tennis player's favored forearm hypertrophies into a clublike appendage, but a barber's less-favored pinkie sometimes atrophies into a digit as limpid as a hair-strand in need of reinforcing-gel to stand erect.

The recoil of a hammer-head's nail-driving momentum
and the backlash of a hammer-claw's nail-pulling impetus
meet at a midpoint
where a fore-armed and five-fingered hand
finds itself suspended between Doing and Undoing.

※ ※ ※ ※ ※ ※ ※ ※ ※ ※ ※ ※

The superstition that warns us to never trim our fingernails at certain phases of the month seems to assume that there are miniscule moon-spirits animating the lunar crescent of our cuticles. An old German superstition contends that trimming a child's nails before the age of one year will produce a stutterer, but makes no mention of hand-lotion aiding in the development of silken-tongued eloquence.

The wind caused by a punch missing its mark
    can howl like a zephyr
        or moan like a Santa Ana
            or whistle like a panhandle cyclone,
depending on the cause, aim, and location of the fisticuffs in question.

Data companies who are patenting hand-gestures like screen-scrolling and pinching-to-zoom are infringing on the entitlements and autonomy of our extremities.

When trying to retrieve a word momentarily
        lost from our vocabulary,
           our hand-gestures grasp vagrant vowels
              out of the ether,
            pry stubborn consonants
         loose from hidden mental crannies,
               and clap syllables into being like a thundercloud.

                    8888888888888888888888

Our hand fallen asleep and dreaming
of hurling a javelin into the flank of a bison
is like a domesticated dog dreaming
of his lapsed membership in the primeval wolf-pack
or a bodega tabby-cat dreaming
of blending his stripes with the high grass of the Serengeti plain.

There are historic, highly prized diamonds that seem to curse every hand that ever owns them with bad fortune, like hexagons that take their "hex-" too literally or a bauble able to blink its own fly-faceted evil eye.

Sometimes the hand merely "presses" a silence-button
or "turns" an off-knob
and sometimes it "flips" a kill-switch
or "slams" a dead-man's lever
depending on how emphatic
the exit from a particular appliance is.

If our body-parts earned their own reincarnation, some bodies' hands would reincarnate backward as fins even as their corresponding feet reincarnated forward as wheels.

****

Sheep are bred short-legged to prevent them from jumping over farm-fences and gaining their freedom and humans are (by now) bred short-armed (by primate standards) to prevent them from knuckle-walking and recuperating their apehood.

If a particularly motivated middle finger is indeed a "bird"
certain people's obscene gestures
(depending on their level of emphasis)
are more shotgun-avoiding pheasant than cutlery-avoiding turkey
or more wind-gliding albatross than formation-favoring goose.

A good maître-de seats couples within a group at the corners of large tables so that their hands can still graze and grasp, allowing proximity and angularity to join forces in the geometry-dependent dance of courtship.

When half of an ovation's handclaps miss their mark,
the word "fan" means "appreciator"
and "wind-generator" at the same time.

Some classical Chinese painters used a fingerprint as a signature on a finished canvas, a fingerprint that was occasionally mistaken for a vine spiraling up a banyan tree or a whirlpool at the base of a mountain waterfall, depending on the finger in question.

The transition between pointing
an index finger of accusation
and raising a middle finger of insolence
is a gear that is easy to grind when the clutch of temperament
and the brake-pedal of oncoming circumstance
refuse to coordinate.

If the curled undersides of our knuckles are a fist's version of a lap that disappears when that fist stands up and opens its palm, an open-palm slap can't afford to cross its legs or touch its toes.

Early Freudian analysts used their hands to knit
instead of taking notes while listening to their patients
producing many an agoraphobic quilt
narcissistic beret, codependent tea-cozy
and Oedipal scarf
depending on the analysis being undertaken.

.·|·.·|·.·|·.·|·.·|·.·|·.·|·.·|·.·|·.·|·.·|·.·|·.·.

The barbed-wire harp that Salvador Dalí made for Harpo Marx is an Icon of Impracticality on par with Man Ray's spike-studded clothes-iron and Marcel Duchamp's stool-mounted bicycle wheel, telling the hand that "Use Me" is not an art-object's prime imperative.

Some cultures count manually by lowering and closing the fingers
from an otherwise open hand
instead of raising and opening the fingers
from an otherwise closed one
so that removing is a form of addition
and raising is a form of subtraction
in an arithmetic of increasing-by-disappearing
and losing-by-growing.

The human hand admires and appreciates how the QWERTY keyboard has now lasted longer than many hereditary dynasties and royal houses, bypassing the need for an insignia by serving as its own coat of arms.

"Empty-handed" and "bare-handed"
    are very different states of being
        both in terms of possession and prosecution
while "offhanded" is frequently an alibi
    to lessen accusations against "underhanded."

∧∧∧∧∧∧∧∧∧∧∧∧∧∧∧∧∧∧∧∧∧∧∧∧∧∧∧

The index finger eagerly wetted to turn the page of a suspense novel looks at the protective rubber thimble used for sewing with a sneer of inter-finger and inter-function disdain.

If certain hand-gestures have regional accents,
    some drawl by placing their thumbs inside their belt-loops
    some unround their vowels by jabbing their index-fingers
    and some roll their r's by drumming their fingers on a service-counter.

The hand-tremors of a tequila hangover are generally less intense than those of a vodka hangover, but not because a cactus bears a closer resemblance to a human hand than a potato does or because a potato's eyes flinch at the prospect of a cactus' needles.

The "Door Close" button on an elevator control panel
    tends to be more thumb-worn
        than its "Door Open" button
because the human wish to embark
    is often more frantic than the wish to arrive
        and its desire to exclude
too often more adamant than its desire to invite.

◻◻◻◻◻◻◻◻◻◻◻◻◻◻◻◻◻◻◻◻◻◻◻◻◻◻◻◻◻◻

To drastically rephrase the Book of Jeremiah: the fathers have grappled with the grapes and now the children's fingertips are stained purple, or the mothers have planted on desert soil and now the children's fingertips suffer from dry and scaly psoriasis, or the descendants have learned to breast-stroke, and the ancestors can no longer part seas.

The hand knows that a battery brownout
    is to the juggling of chainsaws
        as asbestos gloves are to the juggling of lit tiki-torches
    and a renewed Cuban embargo
        is to the juggling of sharp-cornered cigar boxes
           and a plastics-recycling plant is
    to the juggling of broken glass bottles.

When our hands are our first-responder to a bodily crisis
   the pinkie is the siren shrieking in agitation
     the index finger is the hydraulic ladder ready to be erected
  and the thumb is the base-camp offering steady advice.

    The white-gloved vocabulary of a crossing-guard waxes emphatic for the imperatives of summoning-forward and staying-put, blinks like an ellipsis with its flashing palm, and plants an exclamation mark like a scepter with its STOP-paddle.

≈∞≈∞≈∞≈∞≈∞≈∞≈∞≈∞≈∞≈∞

The human hand is a vast and sovereign continent to a microbe,
   with a thumb that is a promontory of a peninsula
    and a pinkie that is a dinghy-docking jetty
   and a middle finger that is a missile-silo rocket-launcher.

    The Bible-reader whose hands bring the Book of Genesis to steady eye level is looking for an entrance-ramp as surely as the reader who holds the Book of Revelation at trembling arm's-length is looking for an exit-strategy.

Do two palms pressed together in prayer most closely resemble applause frozen in mid-clap or a book closed on its exact mid-point or a bodily blueprint for a steeple yet to be erected?

If a raised freckle on the lifeline of the hand
    is a speed-bump placed by the roadworkers of Destiny
        a smallpox scar on the loveline
            is a pothole overlooked by the repair-crew of Fate.

«±«±«±«±«±«±«±±«±«±«±«±«±«±«±«±«

If Cinderella dropped her glove instead of her slipper at a masquerade ball as she arrived rather than fled, more fairy-tales would be exercises in finger-popping rather than excuses for foot-binding.

The hands that form into impromptu binoculars
    to peer into the distance
      can begin to suffer from delusions of all-seeing omniscience
        only if hands that form into a temporary megaphone
    agree to suffer from delusions of all-saying Esperanto.

If Einstein's hands had been those of a pianist instead of a violinist, would the General Theory of Relativity be less gravitational in its sense of glissando and more atomic in its sense of arpeggio?

From the inside of an "I Want You" army-recruitment poster
   Uncle Sam's index finger is pressing up against the fourth wall
      of Propaganda, Pugnaciousness, and Patriotism all at once.

ʃʃʃ

When Lord Shiva folds his ten arms into five pairs and crosses his 100 fingers all at once, his self-reassurance has been quintupled and good luck has been increased by a factor of 50. Fortunately for the monotheistic, which pinkie is at the bottom when the hands are clasped in prayer has no effect on which god's hotline is being summoned.

   If paper money's denomination
      affected its rate of speed passing from hand to hand,
         a dollar-bill would be a sprinter and a five-spot a miler
           a sawbuck would be a middle-distance runner
             and a bearer-bond a marathoner.

The Healer's Hand icon of Native America features a spiral on a palm and is a solar hieroglyph and an implied induction coil at once, a restorative curlicue and a palliative corkscrew suggesting that good medicine moves like an orbit instead of an arrow.

To be "all thumbs" is to be clumsy,
    but "all pinkies" does not refer to excessive elegance
any more than "all index fingers" refers to the domineering class
    or "all ring fingers" to serial divorcées.

※:※:※:※:※:※:※:※:※:※:※:※:※:※:※:※:※:※:

In Renaissance plays, the Vice/Villain figure is frequently named Ambidexter and is double-handed as well as underhanded, batting from both sides of the dramatic plate and pitching from both the base and the peak of the dramatic mound.

If our nerve-ends tell us more about our hands
    than about the objects they touch
        this is a matter of an apparatus overriding its own intake
            a device drowning out its own data
                and a lens letting its own lamination do the looking.

In Reiki massage, a therapist treats a patient not by kneading or rubbing but by stationary positioning, using the hand not as a skincomber or a knot-probe but as a transmitter wand and an orgone pipeline.

Only the thumb has the ability to go tip-to-tip
  with every other fingertip,
    giving it a kind of ambassadorial eminence
      and eclectic interactivity
that can undermine the index finger's egoism and imperialism.

§§§§§§§§§§§§§§§§§§§§§§§§§§§§§§§

If a bracelet is a belt and a ring is a collar
in the hand's microcosmic wardrobe
a fingerless lace glove is a camisole
worn in place of the more-modest muumuu of a mitten
 and a set of brass knuckles aspires
to the museum-and-manor status of a suit of armor.

The cell-phone keypad has granted the thumbs—previously limited to spacebar duty on a typewriter—a whole new range of expressive functions, thus promoting this underdog digit to a role more executive and less adamantly opposable than ever before.

The beckoning sign is a scratch on the palm in certain European nations, blurring the line between "invitation" and "itch." The "okay" finger-sign in the West is obscene in both Iran and Brazil, blurring the line between "all's-well" and "orifice."

> Because an upraised palm can apologize as well as an alibi
> and express exasperation as well as an empty stomach
> it is a dust-jacket for our sense of duty
> a foreword for our failed lies
> and a glossary for our gut's innate sense of guilt.

++++++++++++++++++++++++++++

The "Bellamy salute" named for and designed by the man who wrote the U.S. Pledge of Allegiance was eventually retired for being the same as a certain Fascist salute, replaced by our current salute that looks like someone clutching a chest-pain.

> A sleepwalker's extended-forward hands
> feeling for furniture to fend off
> are in a kind of figurative finger-feud
> with a zombie's raised-outward hands
> feeling for flesh on which to feed.

On a stepladder
"rung" isn't the past tense of "ring":
On a handrail
"grip" is sometimes the impossible tense of "grease":
During a cartwheel
"fingertip" is both the past and the future tense of "foot."

If Easter Island heads were attached to submerged bodies, their hands would occasionally stand accused of weaving tsunamis out of doldrums, performing chin-ups on the Tropic of Cancer, and commiting acts of volcanic arson all along the Pacific Rim.

A middle-finger gesture
   that takes the idiom "flipping the bird" too literally
      would risk transforming into a sign-language sparrow
         flamboyantly somersaulting
           off the half-sawn nerve-branches of the hand's tree
      or a gestural cormorant divebombing
         into the tidal currents of a wave goodbye.

The hand prevented from slamming an old-fangled phone into its cradle compensates on its cellular with a screen-sweep as dramatic as an opera diva's on-stage demise. The hand that spends too much time smoothing over the wrinkles in a recently made bed often spends too much time wrinkling half-written letters into crumpled balls destined for the wastebasket.

Requesting your check from your waiter by gesturing a checkmark in the air is a bit more punning but no less iconic than requesting that check by pantomiming a wavy signature in the air. The finger-gun placed into one's mouth betokens a deeper exasperation than the one placed at one's temple because of its more interior sense of pseudo-suicide.

    In one benediction sign
        three fingers stand up to represent the Trinity
though which member is ultimately assigned
      the index, middle, or ring finger
          hasn't yet become a matter of papal decree
         palpable crusade, digital Inquisition
              or inter-Trinity dispute.

👉👉👉👉👉👉👉👉

The human hand knows why the rosin a violinist uses on her bow and the chalk a pool hustler uses on his cue relate to the mineral content of the human hand in very different ways. The human hand knows why those old cigarette billboards that blew four cartons of smoke-rings a day did so as hands-free as Venus de Milo pursuing a vow of silence at a sign-language convention.

    The Fibonacci swirl of our fingerprints
reminds us that a spiraling undertow
lurks under even the most solid grip:
The criss-cross patterns of our palm-prints
remind us that even the soundest round of applause
is an exercise in intersecting traffic.

The most frequently used sign-language gesture for "I love you" is fittingly only a lost thumb away from the mano cornuto (or "horned hand") of cuckoldry. In the ancient system of tantric mudras, the thumb is associated with fire, though clearly not for its now-ironic resemblance to a fire extinguisher or a fire hydrant.

> We also have inverted, internal fingerprints
>   on the under-surface of our epidermis
> that would identify us even if we were folded inside-out
>   in the event of our endocrine organs emerging
>   at the expense of our anatomic architecture.

****
****

The Greek moutza gesture of insult does not bother to hold back a single finger but is instead a starburst asterisk of all-in hand-shouting in which each digit is a middle finger multiplied in force by its neighbors.

> How a gravedigger spoons from a bowl of oatmeal
> and how an auto-worker assembles a club sandwich
> reveal how our hands' profession
> trickles down into our more trivial actions.

A fist-like grasp of a pencil almost guarantees a scrawl because it allows too much equality among the fingers, but the lateral tripod grasp demotes the index finger from its place of dictatorial prominence without any orthographic anarchy ensuing.

The Japanese hand-gesture for goodness (*maru*)
forms a circle where the gesture for badness (*batsu*) forms an X
as if the human hand were a convertible game-piece
in some kinetic tic-tac-toe tournament.

ƷoʃoƷoʃoƷoʃoƷoʃoƷoʃoƷoʃoƷoʃoƷoʃ

A rabbi's Kohanim blessing pairs off the index and middle finger and ring finger and pinkie as if they were huddling into teams of opponents in an upcoming Talmudic dispute over which of the fingers most offend the bylaws of the Book of Leviticus.

    The way that a hand grasps a shot-glass
        or clutches a beer-bottle or cradles a brandy-snifter
           can shift and buckle
              in the hurricane winds of diminishing sobriety
                or tremor and undulate
            in the aftershocks of a faultline hangover.

Vito Acconci's *Hand in Mouth* piece, in which the artist forces his fist into his mouth until he gags, feels like a self-imposed karmic retribution for centuries of western art hiding the hand behind the brush and the chisel and the pencil.

If hands had their own heaven
    as an afterlife for extremities it could be
a paradise of plushness prevailing over a nirvana of numbness
    or a Valhalla of victory salutes
vanquishing a Plutonian realm of pencil-pushing.

†††††††††††††††††††††††††††††††

The raised ridges of our fingerprints behave like radial tires to stabilize our grip on wet surfaces, learning to scuttle instead of skid and drift along instead of dig in. Our fingerprints wrinkle in a warm bath to improve our grasp of slippery hygiene-implements like bar soap and shampoo tubes, as if humidity cued the body to focus more on its handling.

Sometimes the hand is a swaying cobra
mesmerized by the flute-music of Temptation
and sometimes it is a fleeing cobra
chased down into its pocket retreat by the mongoose of Regret.

The *wai* gesture of Thailand uses the hands and the lower back and the forehead in a bowing gesture of class humility, but said gesture's name also forms a cross-language pun on English's aggressively interrogative "why."

The hand passively pulled across the letters
    and numbers on a ouija board
      is bypassing the control-panel of counting
        and the circuit-board of spelling
          and allowing the cave-walls of its carpal tunnel
to be carved-on by a prehistoric urge fossilized inside our fingers.

♯♯♯♯♯♯♯♯♯♯♯♯♯♯♯♯♯♯♯♯♯♯♯♯♯♯♯♯

The Parisian caste system is taken by the subliminal handlebars whenever the overhead, self-congratulating handshake of the Tour de France "victory clasp" causes a cyclist in a gold-lamé jumpsuit to resemble a single earring dangling from a French debutante's phantom earlobe.

The animal born without a sense of touch soon dies
    but a body born with a hand's nerve-ends from head to toe
        might expire from overstimulation every bit as early.

Even when having an index finger longer than one's ring finger means assertiveness, inter-digit disputes can often be resolved by middle-finger arbitration.

A food-minded orchestra conductor's hands pull air-taffy
to draw out the sweet resonances of a string section
and chop air-lettuce or air-arugula
to lend the brass bowls of a tympani section more staccato.

::

The human hand can form into a Cup of Diogenes when drinking
and a Sword of Damocles when threatening
and a Pillar of Hercules when standing firm
adapting a new posture with each new circumstance
and embodying a new archetype with each new demand.

Statistically, when grave-robbers don't take an entire body they most frequently take a hand or an arm, leaving the lower limbs behind to develop an Extremity Inferiority Complex.

When a writer in the death-defying Hemingway machismo tradition tries to bring his bicep into his handwriting, he should perhaps realize that life-or-death surgeons often immobilize their arms to make their hand-actions more precise.

A hand can "lie" itself down and "lay" down other objects
sometimes in a single, collapsing-yet-clutching gesture:
A finger can "flaunt" its independence
and "flout" its interdependence
sometimes in an intermingling of bravado and bravura.

∞∞∞∞∞∞∞∞∞∞∞∞∞∞∞∞∞∞∞∞

The finger squeezing the trigger of an overspent pistol
    experiences banality-of-ballistics and firearm-freeze
    and ammunition anticlimax all at once.

Robert Rauschenberg wore out fifteen erasers obliterating his *Erased de Kooning Drawing*, leaving behind hundreds of rubber crumbs that qualify as supplementary micro-sculptures made without the hand's full consent or intent.

The rotating joystick range-of-motion of the thumb is nearly replicated by the second-most-mobile finger, the pinkie, proving just one of the advantages of marginal outsiderhood.

If Id is a grasping palm
    and Ego is a clenched fist
        and Superego a wagging finger
a glove willing to house one but not the others
    is an instrument of imbalance.

In his "Letter to the Blind," Diderot opines that with long enough arms, our human hands could tell us more about the moon than our eyes can, suggesting that our fingertips are lunar land-rovers just waiting to be launched.

The phrase "feet and elbows"
    cannot idiomatically balance out "hands and knees"
        nor "hands on heels" supplement "hands on hips"
            without a yogic feat of spine-flexing virtuosity
                to alter the body's off-the-shelf arrangement.

The hand speaks the same basic language to the elbow that the foot speaks to the knee, though generally with a more-urgent and quite-literal sense of "grip" and a less-emphatic and only-figurative sense of "step."

The upward-cupped hands that accompany an indifferent shrug
are the existential if not the anatomic antithesis
of the cupped hands that accompany a panhandler's plea.

※ ※ ※ ※ ※ ※ ※ ※ ※ ※ ※

The index finger's temple-screw is a gesture of mental instability, though it means "intelligent" (if done clockwise) in Japan, perhaps because such rotation indicates a tightening rather than a loosening of the brain-bolts.

If hand is to podium as foot is to pedestal,
elbow is to oration as knee is to obedience
even though clap is to appreciation as kick is to insolence.

Under capital- C Communist regimes, applause tends to be more staccato, synchronized and unsyncopated, with a clear disdain for the random handclaps of unregulated ovations or the scattered finger-snaps of fern-bar poetry readings.

    Our hands intuitively know that the ten-and-two grip
      on a car's steering wheel
        would be a spin-and-scratch grip
          on a block-party turntable
            and a pueblo-and-post-apocalypse grip
              on an Aztec sundial.

        ᆼᆼᆼᆼᆼᆼᆼᆼᆼᆼᆼᆼᆼᆼᆼᆼᆼᆼᆼᆼ

A punctual hand sewing a parable about parting onto a pillowcase
    periodically gets to pin-prick its own palm into agreement
      but a glad-hander's greetings are so glib
        that his goodbyes become a matter of guesswork.

The human thumb's divergent angle from the index finger, which tops out at ninety degrees, has allowed human history an even greater degree of divergence from other species' evolutionary trajectories. The word "thumb" (like the word "tumor") derives from a root meaning "to swell," and indeed the thumb swells from misplaced hammer-strikes with greater frequency than the other fingers.

The tongue is used more when speaking English than when speaking certain Asian languages, just as the hand is used more when speaking certain Mediterranean languages along the coastline of outer Colloquial or deep inside the vineyards of Vernacular.

When a master chef's sprinkling hand
is stronger than her stirring hand,
   her soups will be more seasoned than saturated
and her gumbos will be more galvanic than grouped together.

****

If a Buddhist monk can train his ears to hear the ash falling off an incense-stick, can he train the plain of his palms to feel the march of a microbe?

Our handwriting's "tone of voice"
   can be adjusted in several different ways:
      tuning one's crossbars into a less-horizontal frequency,
      dotting one's i's with chirps instead of grunts
and using one's loops as rabbit's-ear antennae
         to eavesdrop on one's own pronunciation.

What would require a greater degree of hand-fluency: a back-and-forth volley in a round of one-person badminton, the opening and re-opening of a jar of slippery elm ointment with no access to a hand towel, or a game of solitaire in which face-cards refuse to show their flipsides to anyone they outnumber?

> The human hand emerges
> 	from the depths of a near-bottomless gene pool,
> 	dripping with evolutionary algae
> 	and strands of chromosomal kelp:
> 	a five-rayed fin tracing its own fingers
> 		out of a manual of self-assembling.

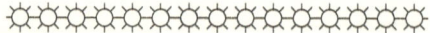

The hand so intricately attuned it can write a prayer on the head of a pin and the hand so amplified it can skywrite "SOS" across several miles of sky understand equally that a two-story tall graffiti mural is the product of an aerosol canister guided by a writer's entire anatomy and not merely by his hand.

> If our rotating thumb
> is operated by a virtual joystick in our brainstem
> the devil's-horns hand gesture
> is operated by a forklift in our hypothalamus.

During arguments, the hand as a relative of the wing knows when to coast on an air-pocket and when to flap to gain altitude. During these same quarrels, the hand as a relative of the fin knows when to paddle against the current and when plunge toward the sea-floor.

If the Pledge of Allegiance requires a hand placed over our heart,
   a vow to never imbibe bootleg gin
should require a protective hand over a besieged liver
  and a promise to never resort to fisticuffs
  should require a labyrinth of interlaced fingers
      clasped like a pacificist maze at the small of the back.

An infant using her fingers to grasp her toes
  is discovering herself as Subject and Object at once:
    hooking up the hardwiring of "I"
  and circuit-boarding the software of "me" in a single gesture.

As we age into adulthood, our fingerprints' personal coat of arms grows in size but maintains its internal ratio and proportion, as if a pebble cast into our gene pool were remote-controlling its own ripples

Ralph Waldo Emerson believed that the truest and most primal of powers keep a permanent finger on their figurative lips, presumably instead of cupping their figurative hands to form a phantom bullhorn to amplify a virtual shout or stomping their allegorical feet on an archetypal curbside to enhance a spectral rage.

If a frog can only see what it eats
and only eat what is capable of moving
what sort of hand can only detect what it fondles
and only fondle what can attempt to escape
and what sort of fist can only locate what it punches
and only punch what can't be otherwise appalled?

^^^^^^^^^^^^^^^^^^^^^^^^^^^

The handle of an Oktoberfest tankard awaits a drinker's grip with a more stalwart and resilient sense of celebration than the elegantly turned tulip-stem of a brandy snifter for reasons that began in the depths of the Black Forest and came to a climax in the post-Napoleonic vineyards of Bordeaux.

If a bobble is a way for a fielder's mitt
    to accidentally emulate a cleated foot's stumble,
  then a fumble is a way for a greased hand
    to emulate a tenderfoot's hobble
    and a wallow is a way for a stubborn hand
      to emulate a foot's unyielding flounder
        and a bungle is a sidelong way
          for a hand to refract a foot's headlong careen.

The Navajo word for "hand"—*ala*—is palindromic, perhaps because in any language, the idea of clapping is a kind of inter-transitive verb in which both hands are each other's subjects and objects at once.

Some gestures are efforts at memory-retrieval
    some at memory-formation
        and some at memory-blockage
depending on whether they are stirring, scooping, or splashing
        the brain's bubbling cauldron.

▫▫▫▫▫▫▫▫▫▫▫▫▫▫▫▫▫▫▫▫▫▫▫▫▫▫▫▫▫▫

There are 15 finger-joints to a standard hand, one for each player on a rugby team, and so a fist is a huddle in which the blind-side flanker and the scrum half and the loose-head prop are in angered agreement.

When a new axe-handle is carved by an axe-blade
    sitting atop an old axe-handle
        the hands of a craftsman have performed a cartwheel
across a hand-tool's spiraling line of genetic transmission.

The hand knows the line between doodling and drawing is fuzzy because the tongue knows the border between muttering and mantra-chanting is often inaudible and the foot knows that the demarcation between a presuming stride and a pratfallen stumble is ever-eroding.

Some painter's hands are most closely assisted
   by the wrist when water-coloring
      by the elbow when working with oils
         and by the shoulder when erasing vigorously.

≈∞≈∞≈∞≈∞≈∞≈∞≈∞≈∞≈∞

If the gypsies are correct and the ten fingers are the ten commandments in sequence, then our left pinkie is about as uncomfortable about being associated with idolatry as our left middle finger is about being beholden to blaspheming, and our right thumb objects to an accusation of murder as vehemently as our right index finger does to being suspected of adultery.

Anti-intuitive advanced actor's workshop assignments:
moan with your hand without relaxing its muscles
grunt with your hand without any sudden movements
shriek with your hand while keeping them below shoulder level.

From a matinee cartoon perspective
a Bible-toting and speedily plummeting sky-diver
knows that the hand that mis-folds its parachute
eventually finds itself alternating
between rapid-fire prayer-sessions and last-minute
    wing-flaps.

The surveillance programs that already spy on our keystrokes know our hand's hesitations and backtrackings and will eventually know our perspiring palms' relative temperature and tremor-patterns.

    «±«±«±«±«±«±±«±«±«±«±«±«±«±«±«

The hand-speed required for the scratching-off of a lottery ticket sometimes rivals the runway speed required for a single-engine plane to achieve liftoff, and with similar motivation. The hand-speed needed for the Whispering Queen card trick sometimes rivals the rotation needed for a multiple-lead-car royal motorcade, for similar purposes of diversion.

If indeed "The hand that gives, gathers"
then by an extrapolated law of alliterating binaries
the hand that collects also compensates
and the hand that harvests also hatches
and the hand that distributes also diminishes.

The difference between a nail-biter and a cliff-hanger
    is a matter of Suspense's gravity on a pair of gripping hands
      a Storyline's twisting of a pair of rotated wrists
      and a Sequel's pull on a set of clinging fingers.

    When a doorknob is capable of polishing its own brass, a passkey is capable of punching in its own combination, and a mini-fridge can mix its own drinks, a hotel is telling our hand to keep its help to itself.

※:※:※:※:※:※:※:※:※:※:※:※:※:※:※:※:※:

A hand is not its partner's "sidekick" for obvious reasons,
    but instead its crony in terms of endurance
      its accomplice in terms of offense
        and its ally in terms of inter-digital diplomacy.

    A writer's hand trying to end-stop a final sentence into formal submission waves off a question mark as too wavering and elbows away an ellipsis as too infinite and puts down a personal period in place of a pawprint.

www.ingramcontent.com/pod-product-compliance
Lightning Source LLC
Chambersburg PA
CBHW030529080526
44586CB00011B/371